Our Five Senses

Nikki Diggory

ROSEN
COMMON CORE
READERS

Rosen
Classroom™

New York

Published in 2013 by The Rosen Publishing Group, Inc.
29 East 21st Street, New York, NY 10010

Book Design: Michael J. Flynn

Photo Credits: Cover Elena Ray/Shutterstock.com; p. amahuron/Shutterstock.com; p. 7 AISPIX/Shutterstock.com;
p. 9 Pete Pahham/Shutterstock.com; p. 11 Dervin Witmer/Shutterstock.com; p. 13 vovan/Shutterstock.com;
p. 15 Mark Herreid/Shutterstock.com.

ISBN: 978-1-4488-8686-9
6-pack ISBN: 978-1-4488-8687-6

Manufactured in the United States of America

CPSIA Compliance Information: Batch #WS12RC: For further information contact Rosen Publishing, New York, New York at 1-800-237-9932.

Word Count: 39

Contents

We use our five senses every day!

I touch a blanket.
It feels soft.

I taste candy.
It tastes sweet.

I smell cookies.
They smell good.

I see the clouds.
They look white.

13

I hear music.
It sounds loud.

Words to Know

blanket

clouds

cookies

Index